Facts About the Little Blue Penguin

By Lisa Strattin

© 2016 Lisa Strattin

Facts for Kids Picture Books by Lisa Strattin

Guanaco, Vol 74

Marine Iguana, Vol 75

Giant Squirrel, Vol 76

Mynah Birds, Vol 77

Red Admiral Butterfly, Vol 78

Star Tortoise, Vol 79

Walking Stick Insect, Vol 80

Shoebill Stork, Vol 81

Jaguarundi, Vol 82

Rhesus Macaque, Vol 83

Sign Up for New Release Emails Here

http://lisastrattin.com/subscribe-here

Join the KidCrafts Monthly Program Here

http://KidCraftsByLisa.com

Table of Contents

INTRODUCTION

The little blue penguin is the smallest penguin in the world. It lives in coastal areas of New Zealand and southern Australia, where it dives into the sea to catch fish. In Australia, the little blue penguin is called the fairy penguin. The name little blue penguin comes from the blue color of this animal's feathers.

COLOR ME

The scientific name of the little blue penguin is Eudyptula minor. Penguins are flightless birds that spend much of their lives in the water. Little blue penguins have special dense, waterproof feathers that help them swim in the water without getting too cold.

CHARACTERISTICS

The little blue penguin is the world's smallest penguin, standing just over a foot high. Little blue penguins are nocturnal and spend the day hiding in burrows. At night, they dive into coastal waters to look for the fish and other marine life on which they feed. However, during molting season, when they shed their old feathers and grow new ones, they do not eat for several weeks and spend their days and nights standing still.

COLOR ME

Little blue penguins are noisy, and each one has a distinct call. They also use different calls for different activities and moods. They are social and they normally mate for life. The male and female form a bonded pair and raise multiple sets of babies together, sharing parenting duties equally.

Like all penguins, little blue penguins cannot fly. They make up for their inability to fly in the air by "flying" under the water. Little blue penguins are excellent swimmers and spend much of their lives in the water. Their dense feathers keep them warm and dry as they dive into the water to search for food.

COLOR ME

APPEARANCE

This penguin gets its name from the blue color of its feathers. They can range in color from medium blue to nearly black. The chin and belly are white, and the bill is dark gray or black. The feet of the little blue penguin are pink on top and blue on the bottom. The coloring of the little blue penguin acts as camouflage. From the bottom, they appear to blend in with the sky. From the top, they blend in with the water.

The special feathers of the little blue penguin help it to swim without getting too cold. While birds that fly normally have around 2500 to 3500 feathers, these penguins have 10,000. The feathers are downy at the bottom and stiff at the top.

COLOR ME

LIFE STAGES

The little blue penguin is the only penguin that can raise two sets of offspring during one breeding season. The female lays two eggs at a time, each weighing about 2 ounces. Normally, 2 or 3 days pass between the laying of the first egg and the laying of the second egg. The male then sits on the eggs while the female goes off to find food. When she comes back, the mother and father penguin take turns keeping the eggs warm until they hatch.

COLOR ME

It takes around 35 days for little blue penguin eggs to hatch. Once hatched, the parents take turns feeding and protecting the chicks. The chicks are born with black down that turns to brown in about 2 weeks. By the time they are 1 month old, the down has been replaced with feathers. By 2 months of age, the chicks are independent. At this time, they can fledge, or leave the nest and set off on their own.

COLOR ME

LIFE SPAN

The average life span of a little blue penguin in the wild is 6 years. In captivity, they can live 20 to 25 years.

COLOR ME

SIZE

The little blue penguin measures 13 to 15 inches when standing. Its weight varies depending on season. When molting, it can lose up to 40 percent of its body weight. The average weight of the little blue penguin in 2 to 3 pounds.

COLOR ME

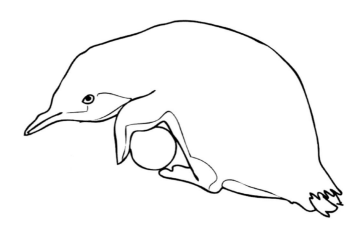

HABITAT

Little blue penguins live in coastal areas of New Zealand and southern Australia. They may live on small islands or on the mainland. They prefer rocky shorelines, and they live in burrows among the rocks.

COLOR ME

DIET

Except for when they are molting or caring for young, little blue penguins fish daily in the shallow coastal water near their homes. They eat a variety of different sea creatures, and their diet changes depending on where they live and what is available at different times of the year. Anchovies, sardines, krill, and small squid are all consumed by little blue penguins. When they catch a small fish, they swallow it under the water. When they catch a fish more than 1 inch in length, they come up to the surface to eat it.

COLOR ME

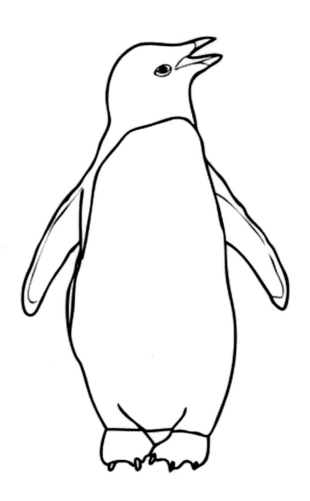

FRIENDS AND ENEMIES

Weasels, foxes, ferrets, cats and dogs all prey on little blue penguins on land. In the water, these penguins may be eaten by fur seals, leopard seals, killer whales, and gulls. However, human activities are the biggest threat to little blue penguin populations. Human urbanization threatens their habitats, and humans also introduce pets and other animals that may prey on little blue penguins. Oil pollution and oil spills can be very dangerous to little blue penguins.

COLOR ME

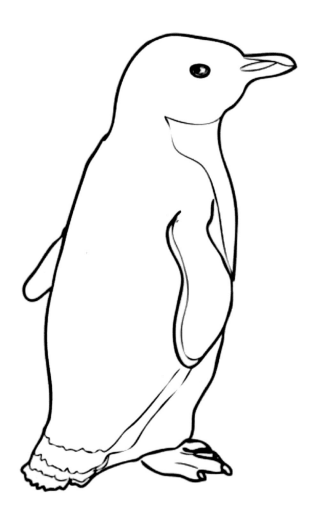

Humans can also sometimes be friends to little blue penguins. Whenever there is an oil spill, volunteers show up to help clean the animals that have been affected. Some concerned people even created the Penguin Jumpers Project. These people put little sweaters on penguins that have been exposed to oil. The sweaters help prevent the penguins from ingesting the oil while they try to clean themselves. Despite oil spills, urbanization, and predation, little blue penguins are still quite common and are not considered endangered or threatened.

COLOR ME

SUITABILITY AS PETS

Like nearly all wild animal species, little blue penguins do not make good pets. They live in a specific environment that is nearly impossible to recreate in even the largest home or yard. They need to be near a large body of water, since they spend much of their time swimming. Little blue penguins are also social and need companionship.

Please leave me a review here:

http://lisastrattin.com/Review-Vol-92

For more Kindle Downloads Visit Lisa Strattin Author Page on Amazon Author Central

http://amazon.com/author/lisastrattin

To see upcoming titles, visit my website at LisaStrattin.com – all books available on kindle!

http://lisastrattin.com

LITTLE BLUE PENGUIN BACKPACK

You can get one by copying and pasting this link
into your browser:
http://lisastrattin.com/PenguinBackpack

KIDCRAFTS MONTHLY SUBSCRIPTION PROGRAM

Receive a Kids Craft and a Lisa Strattin Full Color Paperback Book Each Month in Your Mailbox!

Get yours by copying and pasting this link into your browser

http://KidCraftsByLisa.com

48889074R00021

Made in the USA
San Bernardino, CA
07 May 2017